AF228538

WORLD'S **GREATEST** SOCCER PLAYERS

SportsZone

An Imprint of Abdo Publishing
abdobooks.com

abdobooks.com

Published by Abdo Publishing, a division of ABDO, PO Box 398166, Minneapolis, Minnesota 55439. Copyright © 2020 by Abdo Consulting Group, Inc. International copyrights reserved in all countries. No part of this book may be reproduced in any form without written permission from the publisher. SportsZone™ is a trademark and logo of Abdo Publishing.

Printed in China
082019
012020

Cover Photo: Marcos Mesa Sam Wordley/Shutterstock Images
Interior Photos: Alessandro Di Marco/ANSA/AP Images, 4, 6; Christian Liewig/Sipa USA/ AP Images, 9; Vlada Zhi/Shutterstock Images, 10; Scott Heppell/AP Images, 12; Owen Humphries/PA/AP Images, 15; Victor R. Caivano/AP Images, 16; Fernando Bustamante/AP Images, 19; Manu Fernandez/AP Images, 20; Andres Kudacki/AP Images, 22–23; Kyodo/ AP Images, 24; Martin Rickett/PA Images/Getty Images, 27; Antonio Calanni/AP Images, 28–29

Editor: Patrick Donnelly
Series Designer: Craig Hinton

Library of Congress Control Number: 2019942099

Publisher's Cataloging-in-Publication Data

Names: Nicks, Erin, author.
Title: Cristiano Ronaldo / by Erin Nicks
Description: Minneapolis, Minnesota : Abdo Publishing, 2020 | Series: World's greatest soccer players | Includes online resources and index.
Identifiers: ISBN 9781532190681 (lib. bdg.) | ISBN 9781644943472 (pbk.) | ISBN 9781532176531 (ebook)
Subjects: LCSH: Ronaldo, Cristiano, 1985- --Juvenile literature. | Juventus (Soccer club)--Juvenile literature. | European football--Biography--Juvenile literature. | Soccer players--Biography--Juvenile literature. | Professional athletes--Biography--Juvenile literature.
Classification: DDC 796.3340922--dc23

TABLE OF CONTENTS

THE
BIG KICK

It was April 3, 2018. Cristiano Ronaldo's team, Real Madrid, was facing Juventus in Turin, Italy. The powerhouse clubs were battling in the European Champions League quarterfinals. Ronaldo had already opened the scoring in the third minute, flicking in a goal on a cross from teammate Isco. But no one could have guessed what Ronaldo was about to do in the second half of the match.

In the 64th minute, Real Madrid had the ball in the attacking zone. Dani Carvajal chipped a cross to Ronaldo, who was standing near the penalty spot with his back to

Cristiano Ronaldo had plenty to celebrate when Real Madrid faced Juventus in a rainy 2018 Champions League quarterfinal match.

Ronaldo flipped in midair to blast the ball past Juventus goalkeeper Gianluigi Buffon, *bottom*.

the Juventus net. Suddenly, Ronaldo jumped and began tipping his body backward. When the ball arrived, he smacked it with his right foot, which met the ball high in the air, just in front of the head of a Juventus defender.

The shot rocketed past goalkeeper Gianluigi Buffon and into the net as Ronaldo fell onto his back. The goal gave Real Madrid a commanding 2–0 lead. Even the Juventus fans—who had booed Ronaldo throughout the game—couldn't help being impressed. They jumped out of their seats and applauded the play.

A bicycle kick is one of the most difficult and stunning plays in soccer. Real Madrid coach Zinedine Zidane said Ronaldo's was one of the most beautiful goals in the history of the sport. Fans and fellow players from around the world were amazed by the strike. It was another example of why Ronaldo had long been considered one of the greatest soccer players on the planet.

Ronaldo is one of the world's most popular athletes. He has scored more international goals than any other European player. He has won countless awards, including five Ballon d'Or trophies, given to the best male soccer player in the world. His club teams have captured five Champions League titles. And he led Portugal to victory in the 2016 European Championship.

Ronaldo had also played for two of the most famous and successful clubs in the world: Manchester United in England and Real Madrid of Spain. In the summer of 2018, Ronaldo made it three when he joined Juventus. He had already played 16 seasons as a top-level pro, but he showed no signs of slowing down.

Ronaldo holding the Ballon d'Or trophy has become a familiar sight.

EARLY
LIFE

Cristiano Ronaldo was born February 5, 1985, in Funchal, a city on the island of Madeira, just off the coast of Portugal. Cristiano showed his ability on the soccer field from a young age, and by the time he was 17 years old, he was making his professional debut with Sporting Lisbon's senior team. Ronaldo's strong attacking skills with the ball made him an excellent forward, and he started on the right wing.

By 2003 Ronaldo was already looking to play on a bigger stage. Sporting Lisbon is one of the top clubs in

Funchal is a seaside town on the Portuguese island of Madeira.

Ronaldo got up to speed quickly after joining Manchester United in 2003.

Portugal, but Manchester United of England's Premier League was the biggest team in the world at the time. Ronaldo brought his unique skills and flashy footwork to Manchester, where he became a worldwide superstar.

In his six years with Manchester United, Ronaldo and his teammates continued the club's dominance of English soccer. They won three straight Premier League titles, from 2006–07 through 2008–09. Manchester United also won the League Cup in 2005–06 and 2008–09.

But 2008 topped them all, both for the club and for its young superstar. In addition to its Premier League title, Manchester United won the Champions League, a yearlong competition between the top clubs in Europe. Ronaldo led all players with eight goals in that tournament, including one in the final against Chelsea.

KNUCKLE UNDER

One of Ronaldo's most famous goals with Manchester United came on January 30, 2008, against Portsmouth. He scored on a free kick with a shot known as a knuckleball. This strike is difficult to master. When it's hit properly, the ball spins very little, causing it to zigzag through the air. Keepers have a hard time guessing which way the ball will go, making it difficult to defend. Ronaldo's strike appeared to be heading straight at keeper David James. Then it veered sharply to the right and found the corner of the net.

The victory was only Manchester United's third in the 53-year history of the competition to determine the champions of Europe. Ronaldo also won all the major player of the year awards, including his first Ballon d'Or.

However, bigger things were still to come. Before the start of the 2009–10 season, Spanish giant Real Madrid purchased his rights for a record transfer fee. Madrid fans had high expectations of their club and its players. Ronaldo was about to raise them even higher.

Ronaldo celebrates his goal in the 2008 Champions League final.

bwin
.com
bwin
.com
Realmadrid
Realmadrid
Realmadrid
Realmadrid
Realmadrid

THE MOVE
TO MADRID

Ronaldo had established himself as a global superstar at Manchester United. At Real Madrid, he showed he was one of the best players ever. When Ronaldo arrived in Spain, Real Madrid's rival Barcelona—with its own star, Lionel Messi—was dominating the sport. Behind Ronaldo, Madrid took over. They won the Champions League four times in five years from 2014 to 2018. During that run, they became the first team to win three in a row since the 1970s.

Real Madrid fans packed the famous Santiago Bernabéu stadium for Ronaldo's presentation on July 6, 2009.

Although Madrid had no shortage of talented players, Ronaldo was the centerpiece. He came through in big games, and he often delivered highlight-worthy goals, such as his famous bicycle kick against Juventus.

Another strike that wowed the crowd was a header on April 20, 2011, late in Ronaldo's second season with his new club. Real Madrid was facing Barcelona in the Copa del Rey final. A scoreless game was in extra time when Ronaldo made his move.

Madrid's Angel Di Maria ran down the left wing and sent a high cross to Ronaldo. The Portuguese star leaped into the air and struck like

Ronaldo, *left*, is mobbed by his teammates after his game-winning goal against Barcelona in the 2011 Copa del Rey final.

a cobra. He snapped his neck forward as his head struck the ball, which shot back across the face of the goal and into the top left corner.

European success did not come immediately after Ronaldo arrived in Spain, however. Real Madrid is the most decorated team in Champions League history, but it hadn't won the prestigious competition since 2002. Since then, Messi had led Barcelona to three Champions League titles, the most recent coming in 2011.

Finally, on May 24, 2014, in front of Ronaldo's home fans in Lisbon, Portugal, Real Madrid won its tenth Champions League title with a 4–1 victory over Atlético Madrid. Ronaldo sealed the victory with a late penalty kick, his record seventeenth goal of the tournament. Ronaldo also won his third Ballon d'Or that year.

By October 2015, Ronaldo had become Real Madrid's all-time leading scorer with 325 goals. That effort included five goals in a 9–1 match against Granada—his hat trick was completed in an eight-minute span in the first half.

He became the first player to score 30 goals in six consecutive seasons in La Liga. Ronaldo eventually scored 451 goals in nine seasons with the team, including 44 in 44 games in the 2017–18 schedule. And he led Real Madrid to three more Champions League titles, from 2015–16 to 2017–18, as he and Messi continued their battle over the unofficial title of the best player in the world.

Real Madrid was dominating European soccer. However, Ronaldo was ready for a new challenge. In the summer of 2018, he was on the move once again. It was time to see if he could help rejuvenate another proud club—this time, in Italy.

Ronaldo has used his head to score a lot of goals over the years.

GIVING BACK, GOING ON

When he's not playing soccer, Ronaldo spends time with his family. As one of the most famous athletes in the world, brands have been eager to have him serve as their spokesperson. Nike first signed Ronaldo as a young player in 2003. In 2016 he became the third person to receive a lifetime contract from the company, after Michael Jordan and LeBron James. Ronaldo has other sponsorships with clothing and watch brands. He even has his own app. Some of the app's proceeds go to Save the Children—a charity Ronaldo works with on a regular basis.

Ronaldo works with young players at a soccer school in Japan.

Ronaldo has been recognized as one of the world's most charitable athletes. He donated millions of dollars in aid to Nepal after an earthquake devastated the country in April 2015. Two years later, he funded the building of a children's hospital in Santiago, Chile. The same year, he also auctioned a replica of his 2013 Ballon d'Or trophy with all proceeds going to the Make-A-Wish Foundation.

After his mother was diagnosed with cancer, Ronaldo gave $165,000 in 2009 to the Portuguese hospital that treated her. That money helped fund a new cancer center on the site.

On the field, Ronaldo joined Juventus after another big-money transfer in July 2018. The club, based in Turin, Italy, has a rich history in Italian and European soccer. Juventus had won the previous seven titles in Italy's top league, Serie A. But it hadn't won

Ronaldo returned to Old Trafford, Manchester United's famed stadium, with Juventus for a Champions League match in 2018.

a Champions League title since 1996 and had lost to Ronaldo's Real Madrid team in the 2017 final.

Ronaldo set about changing that in his first year, but Juventus came up short, losing to Dutch club Ajax in a Champions League quarterfinal upset. However, with 21 goals in league play, he helped Juventus win its eighth straight Serie A title. That made him the first player ever to win a league championship in England, Spain, and Italy.

Ronaldo was part of another league championship team in his first season with Juventus.

GLOSSARY

Ballon d'Or
An annual award voted on by soccer journalists and given to the best male player in the world.

cross
A passing attempt from the side of the field to the middle, usually in front of the goal.

hat trick
Three goals scored by one player in a single game.

header
Hitting the ball with the head.

left wing
The left side of the field.

penalty spot
A small circle 12 yards in front of the goal where the ball is placed for a penalty kick.

prestigious
Worthy of great respect.

rejuvenate
Provide new energy.

rival
An opponent with whom a player or team has a fierce and ongoing competition.

strike
To kick the ball.

transfer fee
The amount of money paid by one club to another for the right to sign one of their players to a contract.

MORE INFORMATION

BOOKS

Apps, Roy. *Sporting Heroes: Cristiano Ronaldo*. London, UK: Franklin Watts, 2017.

Bader, Bonnie. *What Is the World Cup?* New York: Penguin Workshop, 2018.

Kortemeier, Todd. *Real Madrid CF*. Minneapolis, MN: Abdo Publishing, 2018.

ONLINE RESOURCES

To learn more about Cristiano Ronaldo, please visit **abdobooklinks.com** or scan this QR code. These links are routinely monitored and updated to provide the most current information available.

INDEX

ABOUT THE AUTHOR

Erin Nicks is from Thunder Bay, Ontario. She has written about sports for newspapers and websites for the past 20 years. She currently lives in Ottawa, Ontario.